This book belongs to

_____

_____

_____

" I always believe I can be the best, achieve the best,
I always see myself in the top position. "

SERENA WILLIAMS

" When you do something best in life, you don't really
want to give that up — and for me it's tennis. "

ROGER FEDERER

" Competing or just for fun, whatever,
simply enjoy and try your best. "

RAFAEL NADAL

" You have to consistently be successful to be one
of the top players in the world,
and everything is possible in life. "

NOVAK DJOKOVIC

PRE PRACTICE OBJECTIVES

Date: _____

Today's Area of focus (Technical or Tactical)

1. _____

2. _____

POST PRACTICE EVALUATION

Attitude Scale (1-5):   ◯ ◯ ◯ ◯ ◯

Engagement Levels (1-5): ◯ ◯ ◯ ◯ ◯

Energy Levels (1-5):   ◯ ◯ ◯ ◯ ◯

Lessons Learned

_____

_____

_____

Coach's Comments

_____

_____

_____

PRE PRACTICE OBJECTIVES

Date: _____

Today's Area of focus (Technical or Tactical)

1. _____

2. _____

POST PRACTICE EVALUATION

Attitude Scale (1-5):   ⚾ ⚾ ⚾ ⚾ ⚾

Engagement Levels (1-5):   ⚾ ⚾ ⚾ ⚾ ⚾

Energy Levels (1-5):   ⚾ ⚾ ⚾ ⚾ ⚾

Lessons Learned

_____

_____

_____

Coach's Comments

_____

_____

_____

PRE PRACTICE OBJECTIVES

Date: _____

Today's Area of focus (Technical or Tactical)

1. _____

2. _____

POST PRACTICE EVALUATION

Attitude Scale (1-5):   ◯◯ ◯◯ ◯◯ ◯◯ ◯◯

Engagement Levels (1-5): ◯◯ ◯◯ ◯◯ ◯◯ ◯◯

Energy Levels (1-5):   ◯◯ ◯◯ ◯◯ ◯◯ ◯◯

Lessons Learned

_____

_____

_____

Coach's Comments

_____

_____

_____

PRE PRACTICE OBJECTIVES

Date: _____

Today's Area of focus (Technical or Tactical)

1. _____

2. _____

POST PRACTICE EVALUATION

Attitude Scale (1-5):   ◯ ◯ ◯ ◯ ◯

Engagement Levels (1-5):   ◯ ◯ ◯ ◯ ◯

Energy Levels (1-5):   ◯ ◯ ◯ ◯ ◯

Lessons Learned

_____

_____

_____

Coach's Comments

_____

_____

_____

PRE PRACTICE OBJECTIVES

Date: _____

Today's Area of focus (Technical or Tactical)

1. _____

2. _____

POST PRACTICE EVALUATION

Attitude Scale (1-5): ◯ ◯ ◯ ◯ ◯

Engagement Levels (1-5): ◯ ◯ ◯ ◯ ◯

Energy Levels (1-5): ◯ ◯ ◯ ◯ ◯

Lessons Learned

_____

_____

_____

Coach's Comments

_____

_____

_____

PRE PRACTICE OBJECTIVES

Date: _____

Today's Area of focus (Technical or Tactical)

1. _____

2. _____

POST PRACTICE EVALUATION

Attitude Scale (1-5):   ◯ ◯ ◯ ◯ ◯

Engagement Levels (1-5):   ◯ ◯ ◯ ◯ ◯

Energy Levels (1-5):   ◯ ◯ ◯ ◯ ◯

Lessons Learned

_____

_____

_____

Coach's Comments

_____

_____

_____

PRE PRACTICE OBJECTIVES

Date: _____

Today's Area of focus (Technical or Tactical)

1. _____

2. _____

POST PRACTICE EVALUATION

Attitude Scale (1-5):   ◯ ◯ ◯ ◯ ◯

Engagement Levels (1-5):   ◯ ◯ ◯ ◯ ◯

Energy Levels (1-5):   ◯ ◯ ◯ ◯ ◯

Lessons Learned

_____

_____

_____

Coach's Comments

_____

_____

_____

PRE PRACTICE OBJECTIVES

Date: _____

Today's Area of focus (Technical or Tactical)

1. _____

2. _____

POST PRACTICE EVALUATION

Attitude Scale (1-5):   ◯ ◯ ◯ ◯ ◯

Engagement Levels (1-5):   ◯ ◯ ◯ ◯ ◯

Energy Levels (1-5):   ◯ ◯ ◯ ◯ ◯

Lessons Learned

_____

_____

_____

Coach's Comments

_____

_____

_____

PRE PRACTICE OBJECTIVES

Date: _____

Today's Area of focus (Technical or Tactical)

1. _____

2. _____

POST PRACTICE EVALUATION

Attitude Scale (1-5):   🎾 🎾 🎾 🎾 🎾

Engagement Levels (1-5): 🎾 🎾 🎾 🎾 🎾

Energy Levels (1-5):   🎾 🎾 🎾 🎾 🎾

Lessons Learned

_____

_____

_____

Coach's Comments

_____

_____

_____

PRE PRACTICE OBJECTIVES

Date: _____

Today's Area of focus (Technical or Tactical)

1. _____

2. _____

POST PRACTICE EVALUATION

Attitude Scale (1-5): ◯ ◯ ◯ ◯ ◯

Engagement Levels (1-5): ◯ ◯ ◯ ◯ ◯

Energy Levels (1-5): ◯ ◯ ◯ ◯ ◯

Lessons Learned

_____

_____

_____

Coach's Comments

_____

_____

_____

PRE PRACTICE OBJECTIVES

Date: _____

Today's Area of focus (Technical or Tactical)

1. _____

2. _____

POST PRACTICE EVALUATION

Attitude Scale (1-5):   ◯ ◯ ◯ ◯ ◯

Engagement Levels (1-5):   ◯ ◯ ◯ ◯ ◯

Energy Levels (1-5):   ◯ ◯ ◯ ◯ ◯

Lessons Learned

_____

_____

_____

Coach's Comments

_____

_____

_____

PRE PRACTICE OBJECTIVES

Date: _____

Today's Area of focus (Technical or Tactical)

1. _____

2. _____

POST PRACTICE EVALUATION

Attitude Scale (1-5):   ◯ ◯ ◯ ◯ ◯

Engagement Levels (1-5): ◯ ◯ ◯ ◯ ◯

Energy Levels (1-5):   ◯ ◯ ◯ ◯ ◯

Lessons Learned

_____

_____

_____

Coach's Comments

_____

_____

_____

PRE PRACTICE OBJECTIVES

Date: _____

Today's Area of focus (Technical or Tactical)

1. _____

2. _____

POST PRACTICE EVALUATION

Attitude Scale (1-5):   ◯ ◯ ◯ ◯ ◯

Engagement Levels (1-5):   ◯ ◯ ◯ ◯ ◯

Energy Levels (1-5):   ◯ ◯ ◯ ◯ ◯

Lessons Learned

_____

_____

_____

Coach's Comments

_____

_____

_____

PRE PRACTICE OBJECTIVES

Date: _____

Today's Area of focus (Technical or Tactical)

1. _____

2. _____

POST PRACTICE EVALUATION

Attitude Scale (1-5):   🎾 🎾 🎾 🎾 🎾

Engagement Levels (1-5):   🎾 🎾 🎾 🎾 🎾

Energy Levels (1-5):   🎾 🎾 🎾 🎾 🎾

Lessons Learned

_____

_____

_____

Coach's Comments

_____

_____

_____

PRE PRACTICE OBJECTIVES

Date: _____

Today's Area of focus (Technical or Tactical)

1. _____

2. _____

POST PRACTICE EVALUATION

Attitude Scale (1-5):   ◖◗ ◖◗ ◖◗ ◖◗ ◖◗

Engagement Levels (1-5):   ◖◗ ◖◗ ◖◗ ◖◗ ◖◗

Energy Levels (1-5):   ◖◗ ◖◗ ◖◗ ◖◗ ◖◗

Lessons Learned

_____

_____

_____

Coach's Comments

_____

_____

_____

PRE PRACTICE OBJECTIVES

Date: _____

Today's Area of focus (Technical or Tactical)

1. _____

2. _____

POST PRACTICE EVALUATION

Attitude Scale (1-5):   🎾 🎾 🎾 🎾 🎾

Engagement Levels (1-5): 🎾 🎾 🎾 🎾 🎾

Energy Levels (1-5):   🎾 🎾 🎾 🎾 🎾

Lessons Learned

_____

_____

_____

Coach's Comments

_____

_____

_____

PRE PRACTICE OBJECTIVES

Date: _____

Today's Area of focus (Technical or Tactical)

1. _____

2. _____

POST PRACTICE EVALUATION

Attitude Scale (1-5):　　　◯ ◯ ◯ ◯ ◯

Engagement Levels (1-5):　◯ ◯ ◯ ◯ ◯

Energy Levels (1-5):　　　◯ ◯ ◯ ◯ ◯

Lessons Learned

_____

_____

_____

Coach's Comments

_____

_____

_____

PRE PRACTICE OBJECTIVES

Date: _____

Today's Area of focus (Technical or Tactical)

1. _____

2. _____

POST PRACTICE EVALUATION

Attitude Scale (1-5):   ◯ ◯ ◯ ◯ ◯

Engagement Levels (1-5): ◯ ◯ ◯ ◯ ◯

Energy Levels (1-5):   ◯ ◯ ◯ ◯ ◯

Lessons Learned

_____

_____

_____

Coach's Comments

_____

_____

_____

PRE PRACTICE OBJECTIVES

Date: _____

Today's Area of focus (Technical or Tactical)

1. _____

2. _____

POST PRACTICE EVALUATION

Attitude Scale (1-5):   ◯ ◯ ◯ ◯ ◯

Engagement Levels (1-5):   ◯ ◯ ◯ ◯ ◯

Energy Levels (1-5):   ◯ ◯ ◯ ◯ ◯

Lessons Learned

_____

_____

_____

Coach's Comments

_____

_____

_____

PRE PRACTICE OBJECTIVES

Date: ______________

Today's Area of focus (Technical or Tactical)

1. ______________________________

2. ______________________________

POST PRACTICE EVALUATION

Attitude Scale (1-5):

Engagement Levels (1-5):

Energy Levels (1-5):

Lessons Learned

____

____

____

Coach's Comments

____

____

____

PRE PRACTICE OBJECTIVES

Date: _____

Today's Area of focus (Technical or Tactical)

1. _____

2. _____

POST PRACTICE EVALUATION

Attitude Scale (1-5):

Engagement Levels (1-5):

Energy Levels (1-5):

Lessons Learned

_____

_____

_____

Coach's Comments

_____

_____

_____

PRE PRACTICE OBJECTIVES

Date: _____

Today's Area of focus (Technical or Tactical)

1. _____

2. _____

POST PRACTICE EVALUATION

Attitude Scale (1-5):   ◯ ◯ ◯ ◯ ◯

Engagement Levels (1-5):   ◯ ◯ ◯ ◯ ◯

Energy Levels (1-5):   ◯ ◯ ◯ ◯ ◯

Lessons Learned

_____

_____

_____

Coach's Comments

_____

_____

_____

PRE PRACTICE OBJECTIVES

Date: _____

Today's Area of focus (Technical or Tactical)

1. _____

2. _____

POST PRACTICE EVALUATION

Attitude Scale (1-5):   ◯ ◯ ◯ ◯ ◯

Engagement Levels (1-5):   ◯ ◯ ◯ ◯ ◯

Energy Levels (1-5):   ◯ ◯ ◯ ◯ ◯

Lessons Learned

_____

_____

_____

Coach's Comments

_____

_____

_____

PRE PRACTICE OBJECTIVES

Date: _____

Today's Area of focus (Technical or Tactical)

1. _____

2. _____

POST PRACTICE EVALUATION

Attitude Scale (1-5):   ⚪ ⚪ ⚪ ⚪ ⚪

Engagement Levels (1-5):   ⚪ ⚪ ⚪ ⚪ ⚪

Energy Levels (1-5):   ⚪ ⚪ ⚪ ⚪ ⚪

Lessons Learned

_____

_____

_____

Coach's Comments

_____

_____

_____

PRE PRACTICE OBJECTIVES

Date: _____

Today's Area of focus (Technical or Tactical)

1. _____

2. _____

POST PRACTICE EVALUATION

Attitude Scale (1-5):   ◯ ◯ ◯ ◯ ◯

Engagement Levels (1-5):   ◯ ◯ ◯ ◯ ◯

Energy Levels (1-5):   ◯ ◯ ◯ ◯ ◯

Lessons Learned

_____

_____

_____

Coach's Comments

_____

_____

_____

PRE PRACTICE OBJECTIVES

Date: _____

Today's Area of focus (Technical or Tactical)

1. _____

2. _____

POST PRACTICE EVALUATION

Attitude Scale (1-5): ⊘ ⊘ ⊘ ⊘ ⊘

Engagement Levels (1-5): ⊘ ⊘ ⊘ ⊘ ⊘

Energy Levels (1-5): ⊘ ⊘ ⊘ ⊘ ⊘

Lessons Learned

_____

_____

_____

Coach's Comments

_____

_____

_____

PRE PRACTICE OBJECTIVES

Date: _____

Today's Area of focus (Technical or Tactical)

1. _____

2. _____

POST PRACTICE EVALUATION

Attitude Scale (1-5):   ◯ ◯ ◯ ◯ ◯

Engagement Levels (1-5): ◯ ◯ ◯ ◯ ◯

Energy Levels (1-5):   ◯ ◯ ◯ ◯ ◯

Lessons Learned

_____

_____

_____

Coach's Comments

_____

_____

_____

PRE PRACTICE OBJECTIVES

Date: _____

Today's Area of focus (Technical or Tactical)

1. _____

2. _____

POST PRACTICE EVALUATION

Attitude Scale (1-5):   ⚪ ⚪ ⚪ ⚪ ⚪

Engagement Levels (1-5):   ⚪ ⚪ ⚪ ⚪ ⚪

Energy Levels (1-5):   ⚪ ⚪ ⚪ ⚪ ⚪

Lessons Learned

_____

_____

_____

Coach's Comments

_____

_____

_____

PRE PRACTICE OBJECTIVES

Date: _____

Today's Area of focus (Technical or Tactical)

1. _____

2. _____

POST PRACTICE EVALUATION

Attitude Scale (1-5):　　　🎾 🎾 🎾 🎾 🎾

Engagement Levels (1-5):　🎾 🎾 🎾 🎾 🎾

Energy Levels (1-5):　　　🎾 🎾 🎾 🎾 🎾

Lessons Learned

_____

_____

_____

Coach's Comments

_____

_____

_____

PRE PRACTICE OBJECTIVES

Date: _____

Today's Area of focus (Technical or Tactical)

1. _____

2. _____

POST PRACTICE EVALUATION

Attitude Scale (1-5):   ◯ ◯ ◯ ◯ ◯

Engagement Levels (1-5):   ◯ ◯ ◯ ◯ ◯

Energy Levels (1-5):   ◯ ◯ ◯ ◯ ◯

Lessons Learned

_____

_____

_____

Coach's Comments

_____

_____

_____

PRE PRACTICE OBJECTIVES

Date: _____

Today's Area of focus (Technical or Tactical)

1. _____

2. _____

POST PRACTICE EVALUATION

Attitude Scale (1-5):   ⊘ ⊘ ⊘ ⊘ ⊘

Engagement Levels (1-5):   ⊘ ⊘ ⊘ ⊘ ⊘

Energy Levels (1-5):   ⊘ ⊘ ⊘ ⊘ ⊘

Lessons Learned

_____

_____

_____

Coach's Comments

_____

_____

_____

PRE PRACTICE OBJECTIVES

Date: _____

Today's Area of focus (Technical or Tactical)

1. _____

2. _____

POST PRACTICE EVALUATION

Attitude Scale (1-5):   ⚬ ⚬ ⚬ ⚬ ⚬

Engagement Levels (1-5):   ⚬ ⚬ ⚬ ⚬ ⚬

Energy Levels (1-5):   ⚬ ⚬ ⚬ ⚬ ⚬

Lessons Learned

_____

_____

_____

Coach's Comments

_____

_____

_____

PRE PRACTICE OBJECTIVES

Date: _____

Today's Area of focus (Technical or Tactical)

1. _____

2. _____

POST PRACTICE EVALUATION

Attitude Scale (1-5):   🎾 🎾 🎾 🎾 🎾

Engagement Levels (1-5):   🎾 🎾 🎾 🎾 🎾

Energy Levels (1-5):   🎾 🎾 🎾 🎾 🎾

Lessons Learned

_____

_____

_____

Coach's Comments

_____

_____

_____

PRE PRACTICE OBJECTIVES

Date: _____

Today's Area of focus (Technical or Tactical)

1. _____

2. _____

POST PRACTICE EVALUATION

Attitude Scale (1-5):   ◯ ◯ ◯ ◯ ◯

Engagement Levels (1-5):   ◯ ◯ ◯ ◯ ◯

Energy Levels (1-5):   ◯ ◯ ◯ ◯ ◯

Lessons Learned

_____

_____

_____

Coach's Comments

_____

_____

_____

PRE PRACTICE OBJECTIVES

Date: _____

Today's Area of focus (Technical or Tactical)

1. _____

2. _____

POST PRACTICE EVALUATION

Attitude Scale (1-5):   ◯ ◯ ◯ ◯ ◯

Engagement Levels (1-5):   ◯ ◯ ◯ ◯ ◯

Energy Levels (1-5):   ◯ ◯ ◯ ◯ ◯

Lessons Learned

_____

_____

_____

Coach's Comments

_____

_____

_____

PRE PRACTICE OBJECTIVES

Date: _____

Today's Area of focus (Technical or Tactical)

1. _____

2. _____

POST PRACTICE EVALUATION

Attitude Scale (1-5):   ◯ ◯ ◯ ◯ ◯

Engagement Levels (1-5): ◯ ◯ ◯ ◯ ◯

Energy Levels (1-5):   ◯ ◯ ◯ ◯ ◯

Lessons Learned

_____

_____

_____

Coach's Comments

_____

_____

_____

PRE PRACTICE OBJECTIVES

Date: _____

Today's Area of focus (Technical or Tactical)

1. _____

2. _____

POST PRACTICE EVALUATION

Attitude Scale (1-5):   ◯ ◯ ◯ ◯ ◯

Engagement Levels (1-5):   ◯ ◯ ◯ ◯ ◯

Energy Levels (1-5):   ◯ ◯ ◯ ◯ ◯

Lessons Learned

_____

_____

_____

Coach's Comments

_____

_____

_____

PRE PRACTICE OBJECTIVES

Date: _____

Today's Area of focus (Technical or Tactical)

1. _____

2. _____

POST PRACTICE EVALUATION

Attitude Scale (1-5):   ⚾ ⚾ ⚾ ⚾ ⚾

Engagement Levels (1-5):   ⚾ ⚾ ⚾ ⚾ ⚾

Energy Levels (1-5):   ⚾ ⚾ ⚾ ⚾ ⚾

Lessons Learned

_____

_____

_____

Coach's Comments

_____

_____

_____

PRE PRACTICE OBJECTIVES

Date: _____

Today's Area of focus (Technical or Tactical)

1. _____

2. _____

POST PRACTICE EVALUATION

Attitude Scale (1-5):   ◯ ◯ ◯ ◯ ◯

Engagement Levels (1-5):   ◯ ◯ ◯ ◯ ◯

Energy Levels (1-5):   ◯ ◯ ◯ ◯ ◯

Lessons Learned

_____

_____

_____

Coach's Comments

_____

_____

_____

PRE PRACTICE OBJECTIVES

Date: _____

Today's Area of focus (Technical or Tactical)

1. _____

2. _____

POST PRACTICE EVALUATION

Attitude Scale (1-5): ◯ ◯ ◯ ◯ ◯

Engagement Levels (1-5): ◯ ◯ ◯ ◯ ◯

Energy Levels (1-5): ◯ ◯ ◯ ◯ ◯

Lessons Learned

_____

_____

_____

Coach's Comments

_____

_____

_____

PRE PRACTICE OBJECTIVES

Date: _____

Today's Area of focus (Technical or Tactical)

1. _____

2. _____

POST PRACTICE EVALUATION

Attitude Scale (1-5):   🎾 🎾 🎾 🎾 🎾

Engagement Levels (1-5):   🎾 🎾 🎾 🎾 🎾

Energy Levels (1-5):   🎾 🎾 🎾 🎾 🎾

Lessons Learned

_____

_____

_____

Coach's Comments

_____

_____

_____

PRE PRACTICE OBJECTIVES

Date: _____

Today's Area of focus (Technical or Tactical)

1. _____

2. _____

POST PRACTICE EVALUATION

Attitude Scale (1-5):   ◯ ◯ ◯ ◯ ◯

Engagement Levels (1-5): ◯ ◯ ◯ ◯ ◯

Energy Levels (1-5):   ◯ ◯ ◯ ◯ ◯

Lessons Learned

_____

_____

_____

Coach's Comments

_____

_____

_____

PRE PRACTICE OBJECTIVES

Date: _____

Today's Area of focus (Technical or Tactical)

1. _____

2. _____

POST PRACTICE EVALUATION

Attitude Scale (1-5):   ⚾ ⚾ ⚾ ⚾ ⚾

Engagement Levels (1-5):   ⚾ ⚾ ⚾ ⚾ ⚾

Energy Levels (1-5):   ⚾ ⚾ ⚾ ⚾ ⚾

Lessons Learned

_____

_____

_____

Coach's Comments

_____

_____

_____

PRE PRACTICE OBJECTIVES

Date: _____

Today's Area of focus (Technical or Tactical)

1. _____

2. _____

POST PRACTICE EVALUATION

Attitude Scale (1-5):   ◯ ◯ ◯ ◯ ◯

Engagement Levels (1-5):   ◯ ◯ ◯ ◯ ◯

Energy Levels (1-5):   ◯ ◯ ◯ ◯ ◯

Lessons Learned

_____

_____

_____

Coach's Comments

_____

_____

_____

PRE PRACTICE OBJECTIVES

Date: _____

Today's Area of focus (Technical or Tactical)

1. _____

2. _____

POST PRACTICE EVALUATION

Attitude Scale (1-5): ⚾ ⚾ ⚾ ⚾ ⚾

Engagement Levels (1-5): ⚾ ⚾ ⚾ ⚾ ⚾

Energy Levels (1-5): ⚾ ⚾ ⚾ ⚾ ⚾

Lessons Learned

_____

_____

_____

Coach's Comments

_____

_____

_____

PRE PRACTICE OBJECTIVES

Date: _____

Today's Area of focus (Technical or Tactical)

1. _____

2. _____

POST PRACTICE EVALUATION

Attitude Scale (1-5):

Engagement Levels (1-5):

Energy Levels (1-5):

Lessons Learned

_____

_____

_____

Coach's Comments

_____

_____

_____

PRE PRACTICE OBJECTIVES

Date: _____

Today's Area of focus (Technical or Tactical)

1. _____

2. _____

POST PRACTICE EVALUATION

Attitude Scale (1-5): ⬤ ⬤ ⬤ ⬤ ⬤

Engagement Levels (1-5): ⬤ ⬤ ⬤ ⬤ ⬤

Energy Levels (1-5): ⬤ ⬤ ⬤ ⬤ ⬤

Lessons Learned

_____

_____

_____

Coach's Comments

_____

_____

_____

PRE PRACTICE OBJECTIVES

Date: _____

Today's Area of focus (Technical or Tactical)

1. _____

2. _____

POST PRACTICE EVALUATION

Attitude Scale (1-5): ◯ ◯ ◯ ◯ ◯

Engagement Levels (1-5): ◯ ◯ ◯ ◯ ◯

Energy Levels (1-5): ◯ ◯ ◯ ◯ ◯

Lessons Learned

_____

_____

_____

Coach's Comments

_____

_____

_____

PRE PRACTICE OBJECTIVES

Date: _____

Today's Area of focus (Technical or Tactical)

1. _____

2. _____

POST PRACTICE EVALUATION

Attitude Scale (1-5):   ⬤ ⬤ ⬤ ⬤ ⬤

Engagement Levels (1-5):   ⬤ ⬤ ⬤ ⬤ ⬤

Energy Levels (1-5):   ⬤ ⬤ ⬤ ⬤ ⬤

Lessons Learned

_____

_____

_____

Coach's Comments

_____

_____

_____

PRE PRACTICE OBJECTIVES

Date: _____

Today's Area of focus (Technical or Tactical)

1. _____

2. _____

POST PRACTICE EVALUATION

Attitude Scale (1-5):   ◯ ◯ ◯ ◯ ◯

Engagement Levels (1-5):   ◯ ◯ ◯ ◯ ◯

Energy Levels (1-5):   ◯ ◯ ◯ ◯ ◯

Lessons Learned

_____

_____

_____

Coach's Comments

_____

_____

_____

PRE PRACTICE OBJECTIVES

Date: _____

Today's Area of focus (Technical or Tactical)

1. _____

2. _____

POST PRACTICE EVALUATION

Attitude Scale (1-5): ◯◯ ◯◯ ◯◯ ◯◯ ◯◯

Engagement Levels (1-5): ◯◯ ◯◯ ◯◯ ◯◯ ◯◯

Energy Levels (1-5): ◯◯ ◯◯ ◯◯ ◯◯ ◯◯

Lessons Learned

_____

_____

_____

Coach's Comments

_____

_____

_____

PRE PRACTICE OBJECTIVES

Date: _____

Today's Area of focus (Technical or Tactical)

1. _____

2. _____

POST PRACTICE EVALUATION

Attitude Scale (1-5):

Engagement Levels (1-5):

Energy Levels (1-5):

Lessons Learned

_____

_____

_____

Coach's Comments

_____

_____

_____

PRE PRACTICE OBJECTIVES

Date: _____

Today's Area of focus (Technical or Tactical)

1. _____

2. _____

POST PRACTICE EVALUATION

Attitude Scale (1-5):   ⚪ ⚪ ⚪ ⚪ ⚪

Engagement Levels (1-5):   ⚪ ⚪ ⚪ ⚪ ⚪

Energy Levels (1-5):   ⚪ ⚪ ⚪ ⚪ ⚪

Lessons Learned

_____

_____

_____

Coach's Comments

_____

_____

_____

PRE PRACTICE OBJECTIVES

Date: _____

Today's Area of focus (Technical or Tactical)

1. _____

2. _____

POST PRACTICE EVALUATION

Attitude Scale (1-5):   ◯ ◯ ◯ ◯ ◯

Engagement Levels (1-5): ◯ ◯ ◯ ◯ ◯

Energy Levels (1-5):   ◯ ◯ ◯ ◯ ◯

Lessons Learned

_____

_____

_____

Coach's Comments

_____

_____

_____

PRE PRACTICE OBJECTIVES

Date: _____

Today's Area of focus (Technical or Tactical)

1. _____

2. _____

POST PRACTICE EVALUATION

Attitude Scale (1-5):　　　◯　◯　◯　◯　◯

Engagement Levels (1-5):　◯　◯　◯　◯　◯

Energy Levels (1-5):　　　◯　◯　◯　◯　◯

Lessons Learned

_____

_____

_____

Coach's Comments

_____

_____

_____

PRE PRACTICE OBJECTIVES

Date: _____

Today's Area of focus (Technical or Tactical)

1. _____

2. _____

POST PRACTICE EVALUATION

Attitude Scale (1-5):   ◯ ◯ ◯ ◯ ◯

Engagement Levels (1-5):   ◯ ◯ ◯ ◯ ◯

Energy Levels (1-5):   ◯ ◯ ◯ ◯ ◯

Lessons Learned

_____

_____

_____

Coach's Comments

_____

_____

_____

PRE PRACTICE OBJECTIVES

Date: _____

Today's Area of focus (Technical or Tactical)

1. _____

2. _____

POST PRACTICE EVALUATION

Attitude Scale (1-5):   ⚾ ⚾ ⚾ ⚾ ⚾

Engagement Levels (1-5):   ⚾ ⚾ ⚾ ⚾ ⚾

Energy Levels (1-5):   ⚾ ⚾ ⚾ ⚾ ⚾

Lessons Learned

_____

_____

_____

Coach's Comments

_____

_____

_____

PRE PRACTICE OBJECTIVES

Date: _____

Today's Area of focus (Technical or Tactical)

1. _____

2. _____

POST PRACTICE EVALUATION

Attitude Scale (1-5):   ◯ ◯ ◯ ◯ ◯

Engagement Levels (1-5):   ◯ ◯ ◯ ◯ ◯

Energy Levels (1-5):   ◯ ◯ ◯ ◯ ◯

Lessons Learned

_____

_____

_____

Coach's Comments

_____

_____

_____

PRE PRACTICE OBJECTIVES

Date: _____

Today's Area of focus (Technical or Tactical)

1. _____

2. _____

POST PRACTICE EVALUATION

Attitude Scale (1-5):

Engagement Levels (1-5):

Energy Levels (1-5):

Lessons Learned

_____

_____

_____

Coach's Comments

_____

_____

_____

PRE PRACTICE OBJECTIVES

Date: _____

Today's Area of focus (Technical or Tactical)

1. _____

2. _____

POST PRACTICE EVALUATION

Attitude Scale (1-5):   ◯ ◯ ◯ ◯ ◯

Engagement Levels (1-5):   ◯ ◯ ◯ ◯ ◯

Energy Levels (1-5):   ◯ ◯ ◯ ◯ ◯

Lessons Learned

_____

_____

_____

Coach's Comments

_____

_____

_____

PRE PRACTICE OBJECTIVES

Date: _____

Today's Area of focus (Technical or Tactical)

1. _____

2. _____

POST PRACTICE EVALUATION

Attitude Scale (1-5):   ◯ ◯ ◯ ◯ ◯

Engagement Levels (1-5):   ◯ ◯ ◯ ◯ ◯

Energy Levels (1-5):   ◯ ◯ ◯ ◯ ◯

Lessons Learned

_____

_____

_____

Coach's Comments

_____

_____

_____

PRE PRACTICE OBJECTIVES

Date: _____

Today's Area of focus (Technical or Tactical)

1. _____

2. _____

POST PRACTICE EVALUATION

Attitude Scale (1-5):   ⚪ ⚪ ⚪ ⚪ ⚪

Engagement Levels (1-5):   ⚪ ⚪ ⚪ ⚪ ⚪

Energy Levels (1-5):   ⚪ ⚪ ⚪ ⚪ ⚪

Lessons Learned

_____

_____

_____

Coach's Comments

_____

_____

_____

PRE PRACTICE OBJECTIVES

Date: _____

Today's Area of focus (Technical or Tactical)

1. _____

2. _____

POST PRACTICE EVALUATION

Attitude Scale (1-5): ⚪ ⚪ ⚪ ⚪ ⚪

Engagement Levels (1-5): ⚪ ⚪ ⚪ ⚪ ⚪

Energy Levels (1-5): ⚪ ⚪ ⚪ ⚪ ⚪

Lessons Learned

_____

_____

_____

Coach's Comments

_____

_____

_____

PRE PRACTICE OBJECTIVES

Date: _____

Today's Area of focus (Technical or Tactical)

1. _____

2. _____

POST PRACTICE EVALUATION

Attitude Scale (1-5):   ◯ ◯ ◯ ◯ ◯

Engagement Levels (1-5):   ◯ ◯ ◯ ◯ ◯

Energy Levels (1-5):   ◯ ◯ ◯ ◯ ◯

Lessons Learned

_____

_____

_____

Coach's Comments

_____

_____

_____

PRE PRACTICE OBJECTIVES

Date: _____

Today's Area of focus (Technical or Tactical)

1. _____

2. _____

POST PRACTICE EVALUATION

Attitude Scale (1-5):   ⊘ ⊘ ⊘ ⊘ ⊘

Engagement Levels (1-5):   ⊘ ⊘ ⊘ ⊘ ⊘

Energy Levels (1-5):   ⊘ ⊘ ⊘ ⊘ ⊘

Lessons Learned

_____

_____

_____

Coach's Comments

_____

_____

_____

PRE PRACTICE OBJECTIVES

Date: _____

Today's Area of focus (Technical or Tactical)

1. _____

2. _____

POST PRACTICE EVALUATION

Attitude Scale (1-5):   ⚪ ⚪ ⚪ ⚪ ⚪

Engagement Levels (1-5):   ⚪ ⚪ ⚪ ⚪ ⚪

Energy Levels (1-5):   ⚪ ⚪ ⚪ ⚪ ⚪

Lessons Learned

_____

_____

_____

Coach's Comments

_____

_____

_____

PRE PRACTICE OBJECTIVES

Date: _____

Today's Area of focus (Technical or Tactical)

1. _____

2. _____

POST PRACTICE EVALUATION

Attitude Scale (1-5):   ⊘ ⊘ ⊘ ⊘ ⊘

Engagement Levels (1-5):   ⊘ ⊘ ⊘ ⊘ ⊘

Energy Levels (1-5):   ⊘ ⊘ ⊘ ⊘ ⊘

Lessons Learned

_____

_____

_____

Coach's Comments

_____

_____

_____

PRE PRACTICE OBJECTIVES

Date: _____

Today's Area of focus (Technical or Tactical)

1. _____

2. _____

POST PRACTICE EVALUATION

Attitude Scale (1-5): ⊘ ⊘ ⊘ ⊘ ⊘

Engagement Levels (1-5): ⊘ ⊘ ⊘ ⊘ ⊘

Energy Levels (1-5): ⊘ ⊘ ⊘ ⊘ ⊘

Lessons Learned

_____

_____

_____

Coach's Comments

_____

_____

_____

PRE PRACTICE OBJECTIVES

Date: _____

Today's Area of focus (Technical or Tactical)

1. _____

2. _____

POST PRACTICE EVALUATION

Attitude Scale (1-5):   ◯ ◯ ◯ ◯ ◯

Engagement Levels (1-5):   ◯ ◯ ◯ ◯ ◯

Energy Levels (1-5):   ◯ ◯ ◯ ◯ ◯

Lessons Learned

_____

_____

_____

Coach's Comments

_____

_____

_____

PRE PRACTICE OBJECTIVES

Date: _____

Today's Area of focus (Technical or Tactical)

1. _____

2. _____

POST PRACTICE EVALUATION

Attitude Scale (1-5): ⚬ ⚬ ⚬ ⚬ ⚬

Engagement Levels (1-5): ⚬ ⚬ ⚬ ⚬ ⚬

Energy Levels (1-5): ⚬ ⚬ ⚬ ⚬ ⚬

Lessons Learned

_____

_____

_____

Coach's Comments

_____

_____

_____

PRE PRACTICE OBJECTIVES

Date: _____

Today's Area of focus (Technical or Tactical)

1. _____

2. _____

POST PRACTICE EVALUATION

Attitude Scale (1-5):   ⚾ ⚾ ⚾ ⚾ ⚾

Engagement Levels (1-5):   ⚾ ⚾ ⚾ ⚾ ⚾

Energy Levels (1-5):   ⚾ ⚾ ⚾ ⚾ ⚾

Lessons Learned

_____

_____

_____

Coach's Comments

_____

_____

_____

PRE PRACTICE OBJECTIVES

Date: _____

Today's Area of focus (Technical or Tactical)

1. _____

2. _____

POST PRACTICE EVALUATION

Attitude Scale (1-5):   ◯ ◯ ◯ ◯ ◯

Engagement Levels (1-5):   ◯ ◯ ◯ ◯ ◯

Energy Levels (1-5):   ◯ ◯ ◯ ◯ ◯

Lessons Learned

_____

_____

_____

Coach's Comments

_____

_____

_____

PRE PRACTICE OBJECTIVES

Date: _____

Today's Area of focus (Technical or Tactical)

1. _____

2. _____

POST PRACTICE EVALUATION

Attitude Scale (1-5):   ◯ ◯ ◯ ◯ ◯

Engagement Levels (1-5):   ◯ ◯ ◯ ◯ ◯

Energy Levels (1-5):   ◯ ◯ ◯ ◯ ◯

Lessons Learned

_____

_____

_____

Coach's Comments

_____

_____

_____

PRE PRACTICE OBJECTIVES

Date: _____

Today's Area of focus (Technical or Tactical)

1. _____

2. _____

POST PRACTICE EVALUATION

Attitude Scale (1-5):

Engagement Levels (1-5):

Energy Levels (1-5):

Lessons Learned

_____

_____

_____

Coach's Comments

_____

_____

_____

PRE PRACTICE OBJECTIVES

Date: _____

Today's Area of focus (Technical or Tactical)

1. _____

2. _____

POST PRACTICE EVALUATION

Attitude Scale (1-5):   ⊕ ⊕ ⊕ ⊕ ⊕

Engagement Levels (1-5): ⊕ ⊕ ⊕ ⊕ ⊕

Energy Levels (1-5):   ⊕ ⊕ ⊕ ⊕ ⊕

Lessons Learned

_____

_____

_____

Coach's Comments

_____

_____

_____

PRE PRACTICE OBJECTIVES

Date: _____

Today's Area of focus (Technical or Tactical)

1. _____

2. _____

POST PRACTICE EVALUATION

Attitude Scale (1-5):   ◯ ◯ ◯ ◯ ◯

Engagement Levels (1-5):   ◯ ◯ ◯ ◯ ◯

Energy Levels (1-5):   ◯ ◯ ◯ ◯ ◯

Lessons Learned

_____

_____

_____

Coach's Comments

_____

_____

_____

PRE PRACTICE OBJECTIVES

Date: _____

Today's Area of focus (Technical or Tactical)

1. _____

2. _____

POST PRACTICE EVALUATION

Attitude Scale (1-5):   ◯ ◯ ◯ ◯ ◯

Engagement Levels (1-5):   ◯ ◯ ◯ ◯ ◯

Energy Levels (1-5):   ◯ ◯ ◯ ◯ ◯

Lessons Learned

_____

_____

_____

Coach's Comments

_____

_____

_____

PRE PRACTICE OBJECTIVES

Date: _____

Today's Area of focus (Technical or Tactical)

1. _____

2. _____

POST PRACTICE EVALUATION

Attitude Scale (1-5):   ◯ ◯ ◯ ◯ ◯

Engagement Levels (1-5): ◯ ◯ ◯ ◯ ◯

Energy Levels (1-5):   ◯ ◯ ◯ ◯ ◯

Lessons Learned

_____

_____

_____

Coach's Comments

_____

_____

_____

PRE PRACTICE OBJECTIVES

Date: _____

Today's Area of focus (Technical or Tactical)

1. _____

2. _____

POST PRACTICE EVALUATION

Attitude Scale (1-5):   ◯ ◯ ◯ ◯ ◯

Engagement Levels (1-5):   ◯ ◯ ◯ ◯ ◯

Energy Levels (1-5):   ◯ ◯ ◯ ◯ ◯

Lessons Learned

_____

_____

_____

Coach's Comments

_____

_____

_____

PRE PRACTICE OBJECTIVES

Date: _____

Today's Area of focus (Technical or Tactical)

1. _____

2. _____

POST PRACTICE EVALUATION

Attitude Scale (1-5):   ◯ ◯ ◯ ◯ ◯

Engagement Levels (1-5):   ◯ ◯ ◯ ◯ ◯

Energy Levels (1-5):   ◯ ◯ ◯ ◯ ◯

Lessons Learned

_____

_____

_____

Coach's Comments

_____

_____

_____

PRE PRACTICE OBJECTIVES

Date: _____

Today's Area of focus (Technical or Tactical)

1. _____

2. _____

POST PRACTICE EVALUATION

Attitude Scale (1-5):   ⊘ ⊘ ⊘ ⊘ ⊘

Engagement Levels (1-5):   ⊘ ⊘ ⊘ ⊘ ⊘

Energy Levels (1-5):   ⊘ ⊘ ⊘ ⊘ ⊘

Lessons Learned

_____

_____

_____

Coach's Comments

_____

_____

_____

PRE PRACTICE OBJECTIVES

Date: _____

Today's Area of focus (Technical or Tactical)

1. _____

2. _____

POST PRACTICE EVALUATION

Attitude Scale (1-5):   ⚪ ⚪ ⚪ ⚪ ⚪

Engagement Levels (1-5): ⚪ ⚪ ⚪ ⚪ ⚪

Energy Levels (1-5):   ⚪ ⚪ ⚪ ⚪ ⚪

Lessons Learned

_____

_____

_____

Coach's Comments

_____

_____

_____

PRE PRACTICE OBJECTIVES

Date: _____

Today's Area of focus (Technical or Tactical)

1. _____

2. _____

POST PRACTICE EVALUATION

Attitude Scale (1-5):   ◯ ◯ ◯ ◯ ◯

Engagement Levels (1-5):   ◯ ◯ ◯ ◯ ◯

Energy Levels (1-5):   ◯ ◯ ◯ ◯ ◯

Lessons Learned

_____

_____

_____

Coach's Comments

_____

_____

_____

PRE PRACTICE OBJECTIVES

Date: _____

Today's Area of focus (Technical or Tactical)

1. _____

2. _____

POST PRACTICE EVALUATION

Attitude Scale (1-5):　　　◯ ◯ ◯ ◯ ◯

Engagement Levels (1-5):　◯ ◯ ◯ ◯ ◯

Energy Levels (1-5):　　　 ◯ ◯ ◯ ◯ ◯

Lessons Learned

_____

_____

_____

Coach's Comments

_____

_____

_____

PRE PRACTICE OBJECTIVES

Date: _____

Today's Area of focus (Technical or Tactical)

1. _____

2. _____

POST PRACTICE EVALUATION

Attitude Scale (1-5):   ◯ ◯ ◯ ◯ ◯

Engagement Levels (1-5):   ◯ ◯ ◯ ◯ ◯

Energy Levels (1-5):   ◯ ◯ ◯ ◯ ◯

Lessons Learned

_____

_____

_____

Coach's Comments

_____

_____

_____

PRE PRACTICE OBJECTIVES

Date: _____

Today's Area of focus (Technical or Tactical)

1. _____

2. _____

POST PRACTICE EVALUATION

Attitude Scale (1-5):   🎾 🎾 🎾 🎾 🎾

Engagement Levels (1-5):   🎾 🎾 🎾 🎾 🎾

Energy Levels (1-5):   🎾 🎾 🎾 🎾 🎾

Lessons Learned

_____

_____

_____

Coach's Comments

_____

_____

_____

PRE PRACTICE OBJECTIVES

Date: _____

Today's Area of focus (Technical or Tactical)

1. _____

2. _____

POST PRACTICE EVALUATION

Attitude Scale (1-5):   ◯ ◯ ◯ ◯ ◯

Engagement Levels (1-5):   ◯ ◯ ◯ ◯ ◯

Energy Levels (1-5):   ◯ ◯ ◯ ◯ ◯

Lessons Learned

_____

_____

_____

Coach's Comments

_____

_____

_____

PRE PRACTICE OBJECTIVES

Date: _____

Today's Area of focus (Technical or Tactical)

1. _____

2. _____

POST PRACTICE EVALUATION

Attitude Scale (1-5):   ◯ ◯ ◯ ◯ ◯

Engagement Levels (1-5):   ◯ ◯ ◯ ◯ ◯

Energy Levels (1-5):   ◯ ◯ ◯ ◯ ◯

Lessons Learned

_____

_____

_____

Coach's Comments

_____

_____

_____

PRE PRACTICE OBJECTIVES

Date: _____

Today's Area of focus (Technical or Tactical)

1. _____

2. _____

POST PRACTICE EVALUATION

Attitude Scale (1-5):   ◯ ◯ ◯ ◯ ◯

Engagement Levels (1-5):   ◯ ◯ ◯ ◯ ◯

Energy Levels (1-5):   ◯ ◯ ◯ ◯ ◯

Lessons Learned

_____

_____

_____

Coach's Comments

_____

_____

_____

PRE PRACTICE OBJECTIVES

Date: _____

Today's Area of focus (Technical or Tactical)

1. _____

2. _____

POST PRACTICE EVALUATION

Attitude Scale (1-5):   ◯ ◯ ◯ ◯ ◯

Engagement Levels (1-5):   ◯ ◯ ◯ ◯ ◯

Energy Levels (1-5):   ◯ ◯ ◯ ◯ ◯

Lessons Learned

_____

_____

_____

Coach's Comments

_____

_____

_____

PRE PRACTICE OBJECTIVES

Date: _____

Today's Area of focus (Technical or Tactical)

1. _____

2. _____

POST PRACTICE EVALUATION

Attitude Scale (1-5):   ◯ ◯ ◯ ◯ ◯

Engagement Levels (1-5):   ◯ ◯ ◯ ◯ ◯

Energy Levels (1-5):   ◯ ◯ ◯ ◯ ◯

Lessons Learned

_____

_____

_____

Coach's Comments

_____

_____

_____

PRE PRACTICE OBJECTIVES

Date: _____

Today's Area of focus (Technical or Tactical)

1. _____

2. _____

POST PRACTICE EVALUATION

Attitude Scale (1-5):   ◯ ◯ ◯ ◯ ◯

Engagement Levels (1-5):   ◯ ◯ ◯ ◯ ◯

Energy Levels (1-5):   ◯ ◯ ◯ ◯ ◯

Lessons Learned

_____

_____

_____

Coach's Comments

_____

_____

_____

PRE PRACTICE OBJECTIVES

Date: _____

Today's Area of focus (Technical or Tactical)

1. _____

2. _____

POST PRACTICE EVALUATION

Attitude Scale (1-5):   ◯ ◯ ◯ ◯ ◯

Engagement Levels (1-5):   ◯ ◯ ◯ ◯ ◯

Energy Levels (1-5):   ◯ ◯ ◯ ◯ ◯

Lessons Learned

_____

_____

_____

Coach's Comments

_____

_____

_____

PRE PRACTICE OBJECTIVES

Date: _____

Today's Area of focus (Technical or Tactical)

1. _____

2. _____

POST PRACTICE EVALUATION

Attitude Scale (1-5):   ⚾ ⚾ ⚾ ⚾ ⚾

Engagement Levels (1-5):   ⚾ ⚾ ⚾ ⚾ ⚾

Energy Levels (1-5):   ⚾ ⚾ ⚾ ⚾ ⚾

Lessons Learned

_____

_____

_____

Coach's Comments

_____

_____

_____

PRE PRACTICE OBJECTIVES

Date: _____

Today's Area of focus (Technical or Tactical)

1. _____

2. _____

POST PRACTICE EVALUATION

Attitude Scale (1-5): ◯ ◯ ◯ ◯ ◯

Engagement Levels (1-5): ◯ ◯ ◯ ◯ ◯

Energy Levels (1-5): ◯ ◯ ◯ ◯ ◯

Lessons Learned

_____

_____

_____

Coach's Comments

_____

_____

_____

PRE PRACTICE OBJECTIVES

Date: _____

Today's Area of focus (Technical or Tactical)

1. _____

2. _____

POST PRACTICE EVALUATION

Attitude Scale (1-5):   ⦇⦈ ⦇⦈ ⦇⦈ ⦇⦈ ⦇⦈

Engagement Levels (1-5):   ⦇⦈ ⦇⦈ ⦇⦈ ⦇⦈ ⦇⦈

Energy Levels (1-5):   ⦇⦈ ⦇⦈ ⦇⦈ ⦇⦈ ⦇⦈

Lessons Learned

_____

_____

_____

Coach's Comments

_____

_____

_____

PRE PRACTICE OBJECTIVES

Date: _____

Today's Area of focus (Technical or Tactical)

1. _____

2. _____

POST PRACTICE EVALUATION

Attitude Scale (1-5):

Engagement Levels (1-5):

Energy Levels (1-5):

Lessons Learned

_____

_____

_____

Coach's Comments

_____

_____

_____

PRE PRACTICE OBJECTIVES

Date: _____

Today's Area of focus (Technical or Tactical)

1. _____

2. _____

POST PRACTICE EVALUATION

Attitude Scale (1-5):   ◯ ◯ ◯ ◯ ◯

Engagement Levels (1-5):   ◯ ◯ ◯ ◯ ◯

Energy Levels (1-5):   ◯ ◯ ◯ ◯ ◯

Lessons Learned

_____

_____

_____

Coach's Comments

_____

_____

_____

PRE PRACTICE OBJECTIVES

Date: _____

Today's Area of focus (Technical or Tactical)

1. _____

2. _____

POST PRACTICE EVALUATION

Attitude Scale (1-5):

Engagement Levels (1-5):

Energy Levels (1-5):

Lessons Learned

_____

_____

_____

Coach's Comments

_____

_____

_____

PRE PRACTICE OBJECTIVES

Date: _____

Today's Area of focus (Technical or Tactical)

1. _____

2. _____

POST PRACTICE EVALUATION

Attitude Scale (1-5):⠀⠀⠀⠀◯◯◯◯◯

Engagement Levels (1-5):⠀⠀◯◯◯◯◯

Energy Levels (1-5):⠀⠀⠀⠀◯◯◯◯◯

Lessons Learned

_____

_____

_____

Coach's Comments

_____

_____

_____

PRE PRACTICE OBJECTIVES

Date: _____

Today's Area of focus (Technical or Tactical)

1. _____

2. _____

POST PRACTICE EVALUATION

Attitude Scale (1-5):   ◯ ◯ ◯ ◯ ◯

Engagement Levels (1-5):   ◯ ◯ ◯ ◯ ◯

Energy Levels (1-5):   ◯ ◯ ◯ ◯ ◯

Lessons Learned

_____

_____

_____

Coach's Comments

_____

_____

_____

PRE PRACTICE OBJECTIVES

Date: _____

Today's Area of focus (Technical or Tactical)

1. _____

2. _____

POST PRACTICE EVALUATION

Attitude Scale (1-5): ◯ ◯ ◯ ◯ ◯

Engagement Levels (1-5): ◯ ◯ ◯ ◯ ◯

Energy Levels (1-5): ◯ ◯ ◯ ◯ ◯

Lessons Learned

_____

_____

_____

Coach's Comments

_____

_____

_____

PRE PRACTICE OBJECTIVES

Date: _____

Today's Area of focus (Technical or Tactical)

1. _____

2. _____

POST PRACTICE EVALUATION

Attitude Scale (1-5): ◉ ◉ ◉ ◉ ◉

Engagement Levels (1-5): ◉ ◉ ◉ ◉ ◉

Energy Levels (1-5): ◉ ◉ ◉ ◉ ◉

Lessons Learned

_____

_____

_____

Coach's Comments

_____

_____

_____

PRE PRACTICE OBJECTIVES

Date: _____

Today's Area of focus (Technical or Tactical)

1. _____

2. _____

POST PRACTICE EVALUATION

Attitude Scale (1-5):   ⚾ ⚾ ⚾ ⚾ ⚾

Engagement Levels (1-5):   ⚾ ⚾ ⚾ ⚾ ⚾

Energy Levels (1-5):   ⚾ ⚾ ⚾ ⚾ ⚾

Lessons Learned

_____

_____

_____

Coach's Comments

_____

_____

_____

PRE PRACTICE OBJECTIVES

Date: _____

Today's Area of focus (Technical or Tactical)

1. _____

2. _____

POST PRACTICE EVALUATION

Attitude Scale (1-5):   ◯ ◯ ◯ ◯ ◯

Engagement Levels (1-5):   ◯ ◯ ◯ ◯ ◯

Energy Levels (1-5):   ◯ ◯ ◯ ◯ ◯

Lessons Learned

_____

_____

_____

Coach's Comments

_____

_____

_____

PRE PRACTICE OBJECTIVES

Date: _____

Today's Area of focus (Technical or Tactical)

1. _____

2. _____

POST PRACTICE EVALUATION

Attitude Scale (1-5):   � ◯ ◯ ◯ ◯ ◯

Engagement Levels (1-5):   ◯ ◯ ◯ ◯ ◯

Energy Levels (1-5):   ◯ ◯ ◯ ◯ ◯

Lessons Learned

_____

_____

_____

Coach's Comments

_____

_____

_____

PRE PRACTICE OBJECTIVES

Date: _____

Today's Area of focus (Technical or Tactical)

1. _____

2. _____

POST PRACTICE EVALUATION

Attitude Scale (1-5):   ⚪ ⚪ ⚪ ⚪ ⚪

Engagement Levels (1-5):   ⚪ ⚪ ⚪ ⚪ ⚪

Energy Levels (1-5):   ⚪ ⚪ ⚪ ⚪ ⚪

Lessons Learned

_____

_____

_____

Coach's Comments

_____

_____

_____

PRE PRACTICE OBJECTIVES

Date: _____

Today's Area of focus (Technical or Tactical)

1. _____

2. _____

POST PRACTICE EVALUATION

Attitude Scale (1-5):   ⊘ ⊘ ⊘ ⊘ ⊘

Engagement Levels (1-5):   ⊘ ⊘ ⊘ ⊘ ⊘

Energy Levels (1-5):   ⊘ ⊘ ⊘ ⊘ ⊘

Lessons Learned

_____

_____

_____

Coach's Comments

_____

_____

_____

PRE PRACTICE OBJECTIVES

Date: _____

Today's Area of focus (Technical or Tactical)

1. _____

2. _____

POST PRACTICE EVALUATION

Attitude Scale (1-5):   ⚾ ⚾ ⚾ ⚾ ⚾

Engagement Levels (1-5):   ⚾ ⚾ ⚾ ⚾ ⚾

Energy Levels (1-5):   ⚾ ⚾ ⚾ ⚾ ⚾

Lessons Learned

_____

_____

_____

Coach's Comments

_____

_____

_____

PRE PRACTICE OBJECTIVES

Date: _____

Today's Area of focus (Technical or Tactical)

1. _____

2. _____

POST PRACTICE EVALUATION

Attitude Scale (1-5):   ◯ ◯ ◯ ◯ ◯

Engagement Levels (1-5):   ◯ ◯ ◯ ◯ ◯

Energy Levels (1-5):   ◯ ◯ ◯ ◯ ◯

Lessons Learned

_____

_____

_____

Coach's Comments

_____

_____

_____

PRE PRACTICE OBJECTIVES

Date: _____

Today's Area of focus (Technical or Tactical)

1. _____

2. _____

POST PRACTICE EVALUATION

Attitude Scale (1-5):   ◯ ◯ ◯ ◯ ◯

Engagement Levels (1-5):   ◯ ◯ ◯ ◯ ◯

Energy Levels (1-5):   ◯ ◯ ◯ ◯ ◯

Lessons Learned

_____

_____

_____

Coach's Comments

_____

_____

_____

PRE PRACTICE OBJECTIVES

Date: _____

Today's Area of focus (Technical or Tactical)

1. _____

2. _____

POST PRACTICE EVALUATION

Attitude Scale (1-5):   ⊘ ⊘ ⊘ ⊘ ⊘

Engagement Levels (1-5):   ⊘ ⊘ ⊘ ⊘ ⊘

Energy Levels (1-5):   ⊘ ⊘ ⊘ ⊘ ⊘

Lessons Learned

_____

_____

_____

Coach's Comments

_____

_____

_____

PRE PRACTICE OBJECTIVES

Date: _____

Today's Area of focus (Technical or Tactical)

1. _____

2. _____

POST PRACTICE EVALUATION

Attitude Scale (1-5): ◯ ◯ ◯ ◯ ◯

Engagement Levels (1-5): ◯ ◯ ◯ ◯ ◯

Energy Levels (1-5): ◯ ◯ ◯ ◯ ◯

Lessons Learned

_____

_____

_____

Coach's Comments

_____

_____

_____

PRE PRACTICE OBJECTIVES

Date: ______________

Today's Area of focus (Technical or Tactical)

1. ____

2. ____

POST PRACTICE EVALUATION

Attitude Scale (1-5):

Engagement Levels (1-5):

Energy Levels (1-5):

Lessons Learned

____

____

____

Coach's Comments

____

____

____

PRE PRACTICE OBJECTIVES

Date: _____

Today's Area of focus (Technical or Tactical)

1. _____

2. _____

POST PRACTICE EVALUATION

Attitude Scale (1-5):　　　◯ ◯ ◯ ◯ ◯

Engagement Levels (1-5):　◯ ◯ ◯ ◯ ◯

Energy Levels (1-5):　　　◯ ◯ ◯ ◯ ◯

Lessons Learned

_____

_____

_____

Coach's Comments

_____

_____

_____

PRE PRACTICE OBJECTIVES

Date: _____

Today's Area of focus (Technical or Tactical)

1. _____

2. _____

POST PRACTICE EVALUATION

Attitude Scale (1-5):   ⚪ ⚪ ⚪ ⚪ ⚪

Engagement Levels (1-5):   ⚪ ⚪ ⚪ ⚪ ⚪

Energy Levels (1-5):   ⚪ ⚪ ⚪ ⚪ ⚪

Lessons Learned

_____

_____

_____

Coach's Comments

_____

_____

_____

PRE PRACTICE OBJECTIVES

Date: _____

Today's Area of focus (Technical or Tactical)

1. _____

2. _____

POST PRACTICE EVALUATION

Attitude Scale (1-5):   ⬤ ⬤ ⬤ ⬤ ⬤

Engagement Levels (1-5):   ⬤ ⬤ ⬤ ⬤ ⬤

Energy Levels (1-5):   ⬤ ⬤ ⬤ ⬤ ⬤

Lessons Learned

_____

_____

_____

Coach's Comments

_____

_____

_____

PRE PRACTICE OBJECTIVES

Date: _____

Today's Area of focus (Technical or Tactical)

1. _____

2. _____

POST PRACTICE EVALUATION

Attitude Scale (1-5):   �◎ ◎ ◎ ◎ ◎

Engagement Levels (1-5):   ◎ ◎ ◎ ◎ ◎

Energy Levels (1-5):   ◎ ◎ ◎ ◎ ◎

Lessons Learned

_____

_____

_____

Coach's Comments

_____

_____

_____

Made in the USA
Middletown, DE
14 July 2023